ANDREW LLOYD WEBBER'S

The
PHANTOM
of the
OPERA

CONTENTS

Music by ANDREW LLOYD WEBBER
Lyrics by CHARLES HART
Additional lyrics by RICHARD STILGOE
Title song: lyrics by CHARLES HART,
Additional lyrics by RICHARD STILGOE & MIKE BATT
Book by RICHARD STILGOE & ANDREW LLOYD WEBBER

The Phantom played by MICHAEL CRAWFORD
Christine played by SARAH BRIGHTMAN   Raoul played by STEVE BARTON

HAL•LEONARD® CORPORATION
7777 W. BLUEMOUND RD. P.O. BOX 13819 MILWAUKEE, WI 53213

Cover artwork by Dewynters Limited, London

World Premiere at Her Majesty's Theatre
Thursday, October 9th, 1986

Visit Hal Leonard Online at
www.halleonard.com

THINK OF ME

Music by ANDREW LLOYD WEBBER
Lyrics by CHARLES HART
Additional Lyrics by RICHARD STILGOE

Viola

ANGEL OF MUSIC

Music by ANDREW LLOYD WEBBER
Lyrics by CHARLES HART
Additional Lyrics by RICHARD STILGOE

THE PHANTOM OF THE OPERA

Viola

Music by ANDREW LLOYD WEBBER
Lyrics by CHARLES HART
Additional Lyrics by RICHARD STILGOE and MIKE BATT

THE MUSIC OF THE NIGHT

Music by ANDREW LLOYD WEBBER
Lyrics by CHARLES HART
Additional Lyrics by RICHARD STILGOE

Viola

7

PRIMA DONNA

Viola

Music by ANDREW LLOYD WEBBER
Lyrics by CHARLES HART
Additional Lyrics by RICHARD STILGOE

Allegro

ALL I ASK OF YOU

Viola

Music by ANDREW LLOYD WEBBER
Lyrics by CHARLES HART
Additional Lyrics by RICHARD STILGOE

MASQUERADE

Viola

Music by ANDREW LLOYD WEBBER
Lyrics by CHARLES HART
Additional Lyrics by RICHARD STILGOE

Poco meno mosso

POINT OF NO RETURN

Music by ANDREW LLOYD WEBBER
Lyrics by CHARLES HART
Additional Lyrics by RICHARD STILGOE

Viola

Andante (♩.)

Allegretto

WISHING YOU WERE SOMEHOW HERE AGAIN

Viola

Music by ANDREW LLOYD WEBBER
Lyrics by CHARLES HART
Additional Lyrics by RICHARD STILGOE